Baby Brontosaurus

by Beth Spanjian
illustrated by Alex Bloch

CHILDRENS PRESS CHOICE
A Longmeadow title selected for educational distribution

ISBN 0-516-09565-X

Manufactured in the United States of America.

102496

It is already mid-morning. The warm tropical sun feels good on Baby Brontosaurus's back. The little dinosaur basks in its warmth, resting his head on his mother's big tail.

Baby Brontosaurus stays close to his mother's side as
the herd of huge dinosaurs moves slowly through the
forest. They stretch their long necks high into the
pine trees and ferns, biting off nearly every needle
and leaf they can reach.

Baby Brontosaurus's neck isn't half as long as his
mother's, but he is determined to reach a very
tasty-looking branch. Stretching his neck as far as
he can, he balances on his hind legs and tail long
enough to get a mouthful of juicy leaves.

Just then, two pesky allosauruses come galloping toward Baby Brontosaurus. The herd immediately senses danger and bands together, pushing Baby Brontosaurus to the center, where he will be safe.

Mother Brontosaurus stands between the attackers and the herd. As the two allosauruses approach, Mother Brontosaurus turns and lashes at them with her long, strong tail. The slender tip whips around and hits the leg of one of the attackers.

As one allosaurus limps away, the other tries to get to
Baby Brontosaurus. But Mother Brontosaurus towers
over the meat-eater. He is really no match for the
thirty-five ton monster and her
powerful tail.

Afraid the attackers might return, Mother Brontosaurus leads Baby Brontosaurus and the others down the river. As they walk, the brontosauruses leave gigantic footprints in the soft earth.

That afternoon, Baby Brontosaurus trots over to one
of his playmates. Making all sorts of noise, the two
little dinosaurs nip playfully at each other.

The two babies haven't noticed the thunderclouds building overhead. With a loud crack, lightning flashes across the sky. The rain pours down and rolls off Baby Brontosaurus's back.

Mother Brontosaurus stops eating and calls out to her youngster. Baby Brontosaurus returns to his mother's side and the two of them follow the rest of the herd into the trees.

As the rain pounds on the spiny fronds above him,
Baby Brontosaurus lies down in the ferns. Tired from
romping, he closes his eyes, and falls fast asleep.

Facts About Baby Brontosaurus

When Did Brontosaurus Live?

Brontosaurus lived in western North America during the late Jurassic Period, about one hundred sixty to one hundred thirty-five million years ago. Better known as brontosaurus, the dinosaur's first and real name is apatosaurus. The dinosaur belonged to a group called the sauropods, which are famous for their long necks, small heads, thick elephant-like legs and long, powerful tails. Scientists used to think the brontosaurus lived in swamps, arguing that its legs couldn't hold up its huge body without the help of water for buoyancy. Today, however, many believe brontosaurus was better suited for dry land and rarely entered water.

What Did Brontosaurus Eat?

Brontosaurus was a peaceful plant-eater, like other sauropods. Once thought to eat only soft water plants, the brontosaurus more likely used its long neck to reach twigs, needles and leaves high in tall pine trees and giant ferns. Some scientists believe the brontosaurus could push itself onto its hind legs and tail to reach branches nearly forty feet high! The brontosaurus ripped off leaves with pencil-sized teeth, but lacked any molars to grind up the vegetation. Instead, with the help of small stones the dinosaur intentionally swallowed, the coarse greenery could be ground up.

How Big Was Brontosaurus?

The sauropods were the largest dinosaurs. Brontosaurus averaged seventy feet long and weighed thirty to forty tons! The dinosaur was fifteen feet high at the hips, and sported a thirty-foot tail and a twenty-foot neck. The brontosaurus had a long, narrow head about the size of a horse's, with its nostril on top of its skull. From far away, the dinosaur would have appeared to have had no head, thus the name apatosaurus (deceptive lizard). Its broad, round, padded feet left prints a yard long and over two feet wide.

What Was A Brontosaurus's Family Like?

Most scientists believe that a baby brontosaurus hatched from an egg the size of a football. Some, however, think that a mother brontosaurus gave live birth to one baby, which may have weighed three hundred pounds! Fossilized footprints show that the brontosaurus traveled in herds at least some of the time. The footprints suggest that the adults protected the defenseless young by keeping them in the center of the herd, relatively safe from attacking meat-eaters.

How Did Brontosaurus Protect Itself?

Brontosaurus was not built for speed and, unlike before, many scientists don't believe it took to water for safety. (After all, the meat-eaters of that time could swim!) Instead, the gigantic dinosaur probably used its long, powerful tail as a deadly whip, slashing any attacker that came too close. The brontosaurus may have even tried to trample intruders, much like today's elephant can. Scientists also think the brontosaurus had good sight, smell and excellent hearing to help detect danger.

Why Did Brontosaurus Disappear?

The brontosaurus disappeared long before the last dinosaurs vanished sixty-five million years ago. Many scientists believe the brontosaurus died out at the end of the Jurassic Period (about one hundred thirty-five million years ago) because of some worldwide disaster that killed off many other dinosaurs as well. A few relatives of the brontosaurus were the only sauropods that survived into the Cretaceous Period.